X

Bibliographical Series
of Supplements to 'British Book News'
on Writers and Their Work

GENERAL EDITOR
Bonamy Dobrée

ENGLISH TRANSLATORS AND TRANSLATIONS

by

J. M. Cohen

PUBLISHED FOR
THE BRITISH COUNCIL
and the NATIONAL BOOK LEAGUE
by LONGMANS, GREEN & CO.

LONGMANS, GREEN & CO. LTD.,
48 Grosvenor Street, London, W.1.
Railway Crescent, Croydon, Victoria, Australia
Auckland, Kingston (Jamaica), Lahore, Nairobi
LONGMANS SOUTHERN AFRICA (PTY) LTD.
Thibault House, Thibault Square, Cape Town,
Johannesburg, Salisbury
LONGMANS OF NIGERIA LTD.
W.R. Industrial Estate, Ikeja
LONGMANS OF GHANA LTD.
Industrial Estate, Ring Road South, Accra
LONGMANS GREEN (FAR EAST) LTD.
443 Lockhart Road, Hong Kong
LONGMANS OF MALAYA LTD.
44 Jalan Ampang, Kuala Lumpur
ORIENT LONGMANS LTD.
Calcutta, Bombay, Madras
Delhi, Hyderabad, Dacca
LONGMANS CANADA LTD.
137 Bond Street, Toronto 2

Ashton-under-Lyne
Public Libraries

First Published in 1962
© J. M. Cohen 1962

117017
820.9/COH   b6204771
7468   6/9

Printed in Great Britain by
F. Mildner & Sons, London, E.C.1

To

E. V. RIEU

In pleasant remembrance of our joint
projects in the last fifteen years

CONTENTS

ILLUSTRATIONS

I. Dr. E. V. Rieu

II. C. K. Scott Moncrieff (1889–1930)
From a portrait by Mercer in the Scottish National Portrait Gallery, showing the translator in the uniform of the King's Own Scottish Borderers (the Edinburgh Regiment) with which he served with distinction in the field

III. Arthur Waley

IV. Constance Garnett (1862–1946)

. . . *between pages* 28 and 29

ENGLISH TRANSLATORS AND
TRANSLATIONS

I

ENGLISH translation has had two great periods of excellence: the first, generally called the Elizabethan though it extends from the reign of Henry VIII until the middle of the 17th century, in which the great works of the Classical past, and some modern books also, were introduced to a country which was from the literary point of view still backward, but whose language was at its freshest and most vigorous; and the second, which began some twenty years ago and still continues, in which English has become and remains the common cultural language of a vast section of the world. Today more copies of the "Odyssey", for example, circulate in English than in any other language, and appearance in an English translation will probably find an author a far wider public than he can hope to reach in his original tongue. Both these great periods of translation coincide with the emergence of a new class of reader in Britain itself. The new rich merchant or landowner of Tudor times, lacking the Latin and French of the medieval noble and cleric, demanded from the new printing-presses the great books of the world in his own tongue; and similarly the new educated classes of our day, whose training has been in the sciences rather than in languages, look to the paper-back industry to give them readable versions of those masterpieces which gather dust on the library shelves until reintroduced in the idiom of their own day.

Every great book demands to be re-translated once in a century, to suit the change in standards and taste of new generations, which will differ radically from those of the past. The Elizabethan translations ignored their author's style and background, intent only on producing a book for their own times; the 18th century made the Classics conform to their own aristocratic standards, ruthlessly pruning away all complexities and digressions that might cause a gentleman's interest to flag; the Victorians conferred on all works alike the brown varnish of antiquarianism; and our own age, in its scientific devotion to simplicity and accuracy, demands plain versions which sacrifice sound to sense, and verbal idiosyncracy to the narrative virtues. It is this preference for plainness that has won our modern translations their wide public in countries where English is only the second language.

II

Up to the 14th Century, the very small body of writers and educated readers in England used Latin and French in preference to the rude tongue of the peasant and citizen. Thomas d'Angleterre, Robert Wace and Marie de France may have written on English soil and certainly treated subjects drawn from English and Welsh history and legend, but which belong to the history of French literature. Geoffrey of Monmouth and John of Salisbury used Latin, and the tradition of Latin writing was very slow to die, since only in the ancient tongue could a writer hope to address a universal audience such as he would today reach with English.

England's first great translator, Geoffrey Chaucer (c.1340–1400), who was also her first great poet, adapted all the leading themes of current Western literature to English uses. Besides acclimatising the ballade, the Boccaccian romance, the *fabliau* or popular story of Flanders, and the animal fable, he translated at least one section—two others are attributed to him—of his century's favourite poem, "The Romaunt of the Rose", and the whole of its favourite work of religious philosophy, Boethius's "De consolatione philosophie", which had been translated into Anglo-Saxon by King Alfred. Chaucer's standard of craftsmanship and accuracy was very high. Indeed a comparison between his description,

in the "Romaunt", of the secret garden as the dreamer first
saw it (lines 135–146) and a prose rendering by a modern
scholar (Brian Woledge: "Penguin Book of French Verse,
I", p. 145) provides the reader with one more reason for
respecting the father of English poetry. Chaucer used
Guillaume de Lorris's original iambic couplet with its four-
beat lines, a measure unnatural to modern English which
more readily adapts itself to the pentameter:

> And when I had a whyle goon,
> I saugh a GARDIN right anoon,
> Ful long and brood, and everydel
> Enclos it was, and walled wel,
> With hye walles embatailled,
> Portrayed without, and wel entailled
> With many riche portraitures;
> And both images and peyntures
> Gan I biholde bisily.
> And I wol telle you, redily,
> Of thilke images the semblaunce,
> As fer as I have remembraunce.

Chaucer takes the liberty of expanding de Lorris's ten lines
to a dozen, and to get the rhyme of his third, fourth and
final couplets crudely anglicises the French words in a way
that would be forbidden to a modern poet. Yet to a reader
with little 13th century French he is almost as good a guide
as Professor Woledge, whose version begins:

> When I had gone a little way, I saw an orchard great and wide,
> all enclosed with a high battlemented wall, painted and carved on
> its outer side with many richly adorned inscriptions . . .

As translator and adaptor, Chaucer laid the foundations
of modern English narrative poetry. But the lyric too
received its original impetus from the translation or adaptation of secular French poetry in the Provençal tradition, and
of Latin hymns. The very early "Sumer Is Icumen In" was
found in a monkish commonplace book which contains no

other poem in English, but many in Latin and French. It is itself an exercise in the Provençal manner, a *reverdie* or spring-song, of which examples occur in every literature that was affected by the Troubadours. An equally beautiful though less well-known short lyric of approximately the same date, "When the Turf is the Tower", appears in its manuscript form directly under its Latin original and the handful of poems that survive by Friar William Herebert (?–1330), the first of our lyrical poets to leave us his name, includes translations from the popular Latin hymns, "Vexilla Regis prodeunt", "Hostis Herodis impie", "Veni creator spiritus", and "Ave Maris Stella", which were no doubt improvised for the purpose of preaching in the vernacular, a custom which was responsible also for the Psalter of the more pedestrian Richard Rolle (c.1300–1349), a contemplative more remarkable for his mystical writing than as a poet.

The most important English translation of the 14th century was, however, the Wyclif Bible of 1384, which reveals all the weaknesses of English prose-writing at that date. Whereas the rhythms of verse, both alliterative and rhymed, exploited the character of the language, those of prose lumbered somewhat unhappily in the wake of Latin rhetoric. The passage from St. John's Gospel which tells of the coming of the Baptist is, in Wyclif's phrases, gracelessly repetitious:

> a man was sente fro god: to whom the name was Ioon/ this man cam into witnessynge that he shulde bere witnessynge of the light. that all men should believe by him./ he was not the light: but that he bere witnessynge of the light· it was verrey lighte the which lighteneth eche man comynge into the world.

Tyndale, the next heretical translator, found in his version of 1534 not only the rhythms which would be followed in the Authorized Version, the greatest of all English translations, but words which were taken over almost unaltered by its translating committee. Where Wyclif's phrasing is abrupt, Tyndale's prose flows in a manner that looks forward to that of the Elizabethans. His repetitions display variety of sentence-structure rather than poverty of language.

> There was a man sent from God, whose name was Iohn. The same cam as a witnes to beare witnes of the lyght, that all men through him myght beleve. He was not that lyght: but to beare witnes of the lyght. That was a true lyght, which lyghteth all man that come into the worlde.

Already, towards the end of the 15th century, the first great era of English translation had begun. The invention of printing vastly increased the supply of books, and widened the circle of potential book-buyers. Malory's "Morte D'Arthur", adapted and printed by Caxton in 1485, must count only partly as a translation, since though based on a number of earlier Arthurian romances, it was freely adapted and expanded. There is as much of Malory in the book as of his original sources. Lord Berners' translation of Froissart's Chronicles, on the other hand, though less well-known, hardly falls behind it in the beauty of its prose. John Bouchier, Lord Berners (c.1469–1533) was a soldier, diplomat and writer with a developed taste for that romantic literature which was so popular at the very moment when the invention of gunpowder and printing was reducing the ideas of chivalry to a picturesque absurdity. Berners not only translated Froissart and the romance of 'Huon of Bordeaux', but also that famous Renaissance forgery "The Golden Book of Marcus Aurelius", or "Relox de Principes" of the Spaniard Antonio de Guevara, whose studied anti-theses, internal rhymes and assonances, and repetitions or doublets, provided the germ for the Euphuistic style of the early Elizabethans. Knowing no Spanish, Berners translated the book from a French translation, a precedent followed by many well-known craftsmen even as late as our present century. Berners wrote a fine flowing style which is even and discursive and equally capable of reciting a battle-roll, of describing the loot, intrigue and destruction of a sordid campaign, and of recording a simple moment with over-tones of mystery that remind one of Malory. Such a moment is that in which Sir John Froissart rides out on a quite un-important journey like one of Arthur's knights embarking on a quest:

> The next day we departed and roode to dyner to Mountgarbell, and so to Ercye, and there we dranke, and by sun setting we came to Ortaise. The knight alighted at his owne lodgynge, and I alighted at the Mone, wher dwelte a squier of the erles, Ernalton de Pyne, who well receyved me, bycause I was of Fraunce. Sir Spayne of Leon went to the castell to therle, and found him in his galarye, for he had dyned a lytell before; for the erles usage was alwayes, that it was hyghe noone or he arose out of his bedde, and I supped ever at midnight.

Berners' Froissart was the first of the great English prose translations, commonly called Elizabethan, which were designed for the ever increasing middle-class which had no knowledge of the original tongues, but a great curiosity, nourished by Renaissance scholarship, to make acquaintance with the great writers of the near and distant past. From Berners' Froissart to the unfinished Rabelais of Sir Thomas Urquhart, from 1525 to 1653, the output of distinguished translations was continuous. In general, the style was exuberant and, judged by present day standards, somewhat marred by the tricks of Euphuism, nouns and adjectives generally appearing in pairs, and by a certain syntactical slackness which renders the connexion between one sentence and the next at times imprecise. Exactness of rendering too, yields on most occasions to a certain leisurely readability. The Elizabethans seem to have designed their translations for reading aloud on winter evenings; their habit of repetition, often so foreign to the original, makes for drowsiness, and at the same time guarantees that the listener will not have dropped far behind if for a moment he closes his eyes.

The Plutarch of Sir Thomas North (1523–1601?), most famous because Shakespeare used it as a source-book for his

Roman plays, was translated not from the Greek, but from the French of Jacques Amyot, and because of this double refraction detail is often blurred that was perfectly clear in the original. An anecdote from the early manhood of Alcibiades, for example, becomes almost legendary in its vagueness when handled by North:

> For they saye there was one Diomedes of Athens, a friend of Alcibiades, and no ill man, who desired once in his life to winne a game at the playes Olympicall. This man being enformed that the Argives had a coche excellently furnished, belonging to the common weale, and knowing that Alcibiades could doe very much in the cittie of Argos, bicause he had many friends in the same; he came to intreate Alcibiades to buye his coche for him. Alcibiades thereupon bought it, but kept it to him selfe, not regarding Diomedes request he had made.

Using almost a hundred words, North entirely loses the dramatic quality of the incident, which Ian Scott-Kilvert, a modern translator[1], captures in no more than eighty-five:

> The story is that there was at Athens a certain Diomedes, a respectable man and a friend of Alcibiades, who was keenly ambitious to win a victory at Olympia. He discovered that there was a racing chariot at Argos which was the property of the city and as he knew that Alcibiades had many friends and was extremely influential there, he persuaded him to buy it. Alcibiades made the purchase for his friend, but then entered the chariot for the race as his own.

The Montaigne of John Florio (1533–1625), which is rated even more highly as a masterpiece of Elizabethan translation, also blurs the hard contours of a style which, though intellectually discursive, is far tauter in its reasoning than its Anglo-Italian translator supposed. Florio does not always use more words than his modern successors. He generally fails however to convey the exactness of Montaigne's descriptions, as in this passage from the essay on Cannibals:

[1] Plutarch: *The Rise and Fall of Athens*. Nine Greek Lives (Penguin Books, 1960).

> After they have long time used and entreated their prisoners well, and with all commodities they can devise, he that is the Master of them; summoning a great assembly of his acquaintance; tieth a corde to one of the prisoners armes, by the end whereof he holds him fast, with some distance from him, for feare he might offend him, and giveth the other arme, bound in like manner, to the dearest friend he hath, and both in the presence of all the assembly kill him with swords.

The actual meaning is more accurately though perhaps less gracefully conveyed in a modern version[1], which renders the manner of the captive's death in concrete language:

> He then ties a rope to one of the prisoner's arms, holding him by the other end, at some yards' distance for fear of being hit; and these two, in front of the whole assembly, despatch him with their swords.

Whereas Plutarch and Montaigne lose their natural outline when clothed in Elizabethan dress, Philemon Holland (1552–1637) seems almost to improve Pliny's "Natural History" by conferring an air of portent and mystery on its farrago of strange information and theory. Despite his Euphuistic doublets, Holland writes a fine, slow-moving prose:

> Not in vaine the planet of the moone is supposed to be a Spirit: for this is it which satisfieth the earth to her content: she it is that in her approach and coming toward, filleth bodies full; and in her retire and going away, emptieth them againe. And hereupon it is, that in her growth, all shelle-fish waxe and encrease; and those creatures which have no blood, them most of all do feele her spirit.

H. Rackham's Loeb translation of 1938 renders Pliny's dubious science more accurately, but could never restore the book to the popularity that it enjoyed in Elizabeth's days. He begins the same passage:

[1] Montaigne: Essays, translated by J. M. Cohen (Penguin Books, 1958).

This is the source of the true conjecture that the moon is rightly believed to be the star of the breath, and that it is this star that saturates the earth and fills bodies by its approach and empties them by its departure.

Even in this version the number of words is twice that of the Latin.

A similar exuberance affects the "Don Quixote" of Thomas Shelton, an Irishman, who translated the first part before Cervantes had finished the second. Shelton, whose Spanish was far from perfect, successfully imitates the tone of Cervantes' voice, even though he misses many of his allusions. Written at a time when English was still rich in proverbs, his version conveys the saltiness of Sancho's speech better than any subsequent attempt. Where he fails to understand a phrase, Shelton unashamedly invents a substitute that generally proves to be quite as good. He is at his best at that moment during Sancho's ill-starred governorship of his Isle when he decides to conceal the fact that he cannot write:

> "I can set to my name", quoth Sancho, "for when I was constable of our town I learned to make certain letters, such as are set to mark trusses of stuff, which they said spelt my name: besides now, I'll feign that my right hand is maimed, and so another shall firm for me; for there's a remedy for everything but death, and since I bear sway I'll do what I list; for, according to the proverb, (*a troop of absurd speeches still in Sancho's part*) He that hath the judge to his father etc, and I am governor, which is more than judge. Ay, ay, let 'em come and play at bo-peep, let 'em backbite me, let 'em come for wool, and I'll send them back shorn; whom God loves, his house is savoury to him, and everyone bears with the rich man's follies. . . ."

Sancho is never-ending, and Shelton can find an equivalent for every one of his homely phrases. A modern translator may ignore all the rest of his predecessors, but is compelled to steal or adapt something from Shelton.

Masterly though Shelton was, he was eclipsed as an inventor of exuberant language by Sir Thomas Urquhart (1611–c.1660), an eccentric Scottish royalist, who left his Rabelais unfinished to be completed by Peter Motteux (1659–1717), a man of less calibre and the first of the professional translators-for-profit. Urquhart was not only capable of matching and freely expanding the French monk's most complicated passages of associative verbiage. He could also write with an exactness that would have been beyond the powers of the Elizabethan translators. His account of the scholastic argument in dumb-show between Panurge and the Englishman correctly describes even the most complicated gestures of the antagonists.

> Everybody then taking heed, and hearkening with great silence, the Englishman lift up on high into the air his two hands severally, clenching in all the tops of his fingers together, after the manner, which, *a la Chinonnese*, they call the hen's arse, and struck the one hand on the other by the nails four several times. Then he, opening them, struck the one with the flat of the other, till it yielded a clashing noise, and that only once. Again, in joining them as before, he struck twice, and afterwards four times in opening them.

Urquhart's directions are sufficient to enable a reader to imitate each one of Panurge's movements. Unfortunately he had no successors. Motteux's completion was a work-a-day job: nor was his "Don Quixote", though far more popular to this day, the equal of Shelton's. The Restoration and 18th Century translator cut and adapted to the taste of his age. Where Shelton's version is longer than Cervantes', Motteux's and its immediate successor Jarvis's are shorter. Allusions and digressions disappear, as does the conversational tone of the original. Motteux and Sir Roger L'Estrange (1616–1704), whose "Visions", an adaptation of Quevedo's "Sueños" was a very popular work in its day, are typical competent practitioners. Dryden, on the other hand, produced a more faithful Plutarch than North's, and Charles Cotton (1630–1668), who wrote Part two of the

"Compleat Angler", comes nearer to Montaigne than Florio, since he writes a clearer and less congested sentence and is free from Euphuism.

Other competent translations which were widely read throughout the 18th century include L'Estrange's *Seneca* and Jeremy Collier's *Meditations* of Marcus Aurelius, both of which played their part in moulding the Stoical character of the educated man of the day. With these works, which belong to the beginning of the century, the first great period of prose translation ends.

III

The great achievements of the Elizabethan translators were in prose. Though the reputation of Chapman's Homer stands high, the work is readable only in extracts. "Judged as a feat of endurance", writes Doctor Tillyard[1], "Chapman's Homer is indeed a prodigy; judged as a poem, the very things that made it a prodigy destroy its value. Bent beneath his labour, Chapman had no strength left to match poetry with poetry." The judgement is not unfair, and is well borne out by the passage which Doctor Tillyard chooses as his illustration, Priam's speech in the last book of the Iliad, in which he begs Achilles to restore Hector's body:

> See in me, O godlike Thetis' sonne,
> Thy aged father, and perhaps even now being outrunne
> With some of my woes, neighbour foes (thou absent) taking
> time
> To do him mischiefe, no meane left to terrifie the crime
> Of his oppression; yet he heares thy graces still survive
> And joyes to heare it, hoping still to see thee safe arrive
> From ruin'd Troy. But I (curst man) of all my race shall live
> To see none living. Fiftie sonnes the Deities did give
> My hopes to live in—all alive when neare our trembling shore
> The Greeke ships harbor'd—and one wombe nineteen of these
> sons bore.

[1] The English Epic and its Background, 1945, p. 359.

Chapman's uses of the rhymed *fourteener* as the equivalent of Homer's hexameter produces, in Matthew Arnold's words, "a jogging rapidity rather than a flowing rapidity".[1] In his "Odyssey", on the other hand, by adopting the rhymed couplet, he exchanged ruggedness for pedestrianism. It was remarkable that an Elizabethan should have the Greek to make this version, but few will greet Chapman's work with the delight of Keats, for each century since Chapman's has produced a better and more Homeric "Iliad" and "Odyssey".

Some other verse translators of the period were faced with less serious problems since the eight-line stanza of their originals was a living measure, which could be written in the tradition of Spenser's nine-line stanza, the measure of "The Faerie Queene". Sir John Harington's version of Ariosto's "Orlando Furioso", Edward Fairfax's of Tasso's "Gerusalemme Liberata", and Sir Richard Fanshawe's of Camoes' "Lusiadas" are all readable substitutes for these three great artificial epics of the Renaissance, and John Sylvester's "Divine Weekes and Works", also, a free translation of du Bartas' "Semaines", which was vastly influential in its day, is in Doctor Tillyard's words "good sound stuff for cut-and-come again reading".[2]

New heights of verse translation were attained by John Dryden (1631–1700) with his version of the "Aeneid", a work attempted by several of his predecessors without conspicuous success. Dryden drew on them all to make Virgil speak, as he says in his "Essay on Translation", "in words such as he would probably have written if he were living and an Englishman". The Restoration poet's easy narrative powers and his mastery of the rhymed iambic couplet gave him advantages that the scrupulous Virgil did not possess. The Roman poet had however a subtlety and richness of meaning which Dryden could not equal with such stock expressions of the day as "his watery way",

[1] On Translating Homer.
[2] Op. cit. p. 353.

"secret springs" and "purple gore". Dryden naturalised Virgil, however, in a translation that frequently attained nobility even though it sometimes lapsed into the vulgarity of what was, compared with the 18th century, an insensitive age. At his best, in that passage from the second book in which the dead Hector appears before Aeneas in a dream, Dryden writes an English epic that is indeed for his age the equivalent of Virgil's:

> 'Twas in the dead of night, when sleep repairs
> Our bodies, worn with toils, or minds, with cares,
> When Hector's ghost before my sight appears:
> A bloody shroud he seemed, and bathed in tears;
> Such as he was, when, by Pelides slain,
> Thessalian coursers dragged him o'er the plain.
> Swoln were his feet, as when the thongs were thrust
> Through the bored holes: his body black with dust:
> Unlike that Hector who returned from toils
> Of war, triumphant in Aeacian spoils;
> Or him, who made the fainting Greeks retire,
> And launched against their navy Phrygian fire.
> His hair and beard stood stiffened with his gore;
> And all the wounds he for his country bore
> Now streamed afresh, and with new purple ran.

Though Dryden did not always capture with his very different talents what he himself called the "exactness and sobriety" of his originals, he went too far when he accused himself of a failure to do justice to Virgil, and said that he believed himself better suited to cope with Homer's "fiery way of writing".[1]

Alexander Pope (1688–1744) certainly failed to catch the fiery quality in the "Iliad" and "Odyssey", but wrote magnificent 18th century poetry. Of this failure he was well aware. While praising Homer as the first of poets in the opening paragraphs of the introduction to his "Iliad", he warns his reader that "our author's work is a wild paradise", which he is setting out to reduce to order. Yet

[1] Letter to Charles Montague, quoted by Tillyard, op. cit. p.481.

when he disclaims all intention of "deviating into the modern manners of expression", one cannot suppress a smile. Pope's age was unpropitious to the epic, and more at home in didactic verse, and it is precisely on its didactic and moralizing sides that Pope's translation is farthest from Homer. Very often, indeed, he loses Homer's immediacy, to achieve only a superbly polished reflection. Yet his rendering of the lines already quoted in Chapman's version certainly conveys the majesty of the poem and a depth of simple emotion even though Priam's grief is expressed in highly formalized language:

> Ah think, thou favour'd of the powers divine!
> Think of thy father's age, and pity mine!
> In me that father's reverend image trace,
> Those silver hairs, that venerable face;
> His trembling limbs, his helpless person see!
> In all my equal, but in misery!
> Yet now, perhaps, some turn of human fate
> Expels him helpless from his peaceful state;
> Think, from some powerful foe thou seest him fly,
> And beg protection with a feeble cry.
> Yet still one comfort in his soul may rise;
> He sees his son still lives to glad his eyes,
> And, hearing, still may hope a better day
> May send him thee, to chase that foe away.
> No comforts to my griefs, no hopes remain,
> The best, the bravest, of my sons are slain!
> Yet what a race! ere Greece to Ilion came,
> The pledge of many a loved and loving dame:
> Nineteen one mother bore—Dead, all are dead!

The build-up is slow, and the climax is perhaps disappointing. Yet the speech has a sustained dignity that entirely escaped Chapman, and that no other verse translator of Homer achieved.

The remainder of the 18th century saw much competent prose translation, but little that was remarkable in verse. Early attempts to render poems from Celtic, Norse and

Oriental tongues were marred by an excess of convention-
ality. MacPherson's *Ossian*, though largely a fake, has more
affinities with Gaelic poetry than Gray's attempts at the
Welsh and the Norse, or the Calcutta judge, Sir William
Jones's (1748–1794) more accurate renderings from the
Persian. Not until the blank-verse Dante of H. F. Cary
(1772–1844), Coleridge's scenes from Schiller's "Wallenstein", and Shelley's fragments from Goethe and Calderón
and the Homeric Hymns is a high standard again attained.

Cary's Dante gives a good and even account of the
"Commedia", which retained currency until displaced by
the *terza rima* versions of Laurence Binyon and Dorothy
Sayers, and Coleridge's "Wallenstein" at times improves
on the stock dramatic rhetoric of the original. Shelley,
however, is of another class. He demonstrates the heights
to which translation can rise when a poet of genius chooses
a work to which he feels attuned. In his scenes from "El
mágico prodigioso" he makes no attempt to reproduce
Calderón's antithetical style. Instead he renders its thought
and imagery with a freedom denied to the Spaniard in his
century of ecclesiastical censorship. In the Daemon's speech,
when he appears, as if escaped from the sea, to renew his
temptation of Cyprian, Shelley translated poetry into
poetry, bridging the hundred and fifty years between the
Baroque and the Romantic by a just equivalence of style:

> DAEMON (aside) It was essential to my purpose
> To wake a tumult on the sapphire ocean,
> That in this unknown form I might at length
> Wipe out the blot of the discomfiture
> Sustained upon the mountain, and assail
> With a new war the soul of Cyprian,
> Forging the instruments of his destruction
> Even from his love and from his wisdom. . . .

The scenes do not reveal themselves as a translation, yet
convey, as Fitzgerald's later adaptations from Calderón do
not, the essence of the Spanish poet's intention. Had Shelley

not devoted himself to original poetry, he might well have been the greatest translator of the 19th century.

IV

The theory of Victorian translation appears from our point of view to have been founded on a fundamental error. The aim was to convey the remoteness both in time and place of the original work by the use of a mock-antique language which was called by William Morris "Wardour Street English", after the fake-antique and theatrical costumiers' shops which were to be found there. The theory was set out by J. H. Newman, brother of the Cardinal, who demanded that "the translator should retain every peculiarity of the original, so far as he is able, with the greater care the more foreign it may be". The Elizabethans had viewed Plutarch, Pliny and Homer as moralists, historians, and story-tellers whose climate of thought and world-picture did not greatly differ from their own. Dress them in Elizabethan costume, and like Macbeth, Julius Caesar or Henry V, they were men of the 16th century. Distance of time and place counted for nothing. The Victorians, by contrast, insisted on it as a prime reality of which the reader must be constantly reminded. A leading exponent of this type of translation was Thomas Carlyle (1795–1881), whose versions of German stories outdo their originals in Teutonic ungainliness of style. But one of the most extreme practitioners was Morris himself, who with his collaborator A. J. Wyatt rendered the Saxon epic "Beowulf" in a language such as English might have been had there been no Norman conquest and no cultural traffic with the Latin world. "Beowulf" certainly presents a special problem. Its language was formal and archaic even at the time when it was first recited. But Morris felt it necessary to stress its antiquity in every line:

> Out then spake Hrothgar; for he to the hall went,
> By the staple a-standing the steep roof he saw
> Shining fair with the gold, and the hand there of Grendel:
> "For this sight that I see to the All-wielder thanks
> Befall now forthwith, for foul evil I bided
> All griefs from this Grendel. . . . "

Even the meaning has become obscure. Much of the antique formality is retained in a twentieth century verse "Beowulf" by C. K. Scott Moncrieff, the translator of Proust. Scott Moncrieff retains the accentual measures and the alliteration, but uses a more modern vocabulary and verse order:

> Hrothgar spake:/ he to the hall going
> Stood on the steps of it,/ saw the steep-pitched roof
> With gold made lovely,/ and Grendel's hand.

The recent prose translation by David Wright[1], on the other hand, goes for the story, remembering that the primitive epic was a tale recited to an audience which could not read, and that, however distant their historical basis, such heroic stories were invariably narrated as if they had happened yesterday. Mr. Wright therefore translated the same passage in this way:

> As he entered the hall Hrothgar paused on the threshold. Seeing the tall golden roof-tree and Grendel's claw, he cried: "For this sight let thanks be at once offered to the Almighty! Much horror and distress I have had to suffer at the hands of Grendel. . . . "

The prose is direct and readable, but retains some hints of the archaism and formality of the work itself. Mr. Wright finds the Scott Moncrieff version "a monument of unreadable ingenuity". His own tells the story, but clearly changes the tone. As he himself says, only Ezra Pound, in his remarkable version of "The Seafarer", actually captures

[1] Penguin Books, 1959.

the real "feel" of old English poetry:

> Days little durable,
> And all arrogance of earthen riches,
> There come now no kings nor Caesars
> Nor gold-giving lords like those gone. . . .

Here the tone is preserved by a free use of the original measure, which is preferable both to the crabbed imitation of the earlier versions and to the plain narrative of David Wright. But Pound's "Seafarer" is an exceptional work, even for him. Most of his other translations, from the Italian and Provençal, are laced with Wardour Street pseudo-antiquities.

The Victorian translator was hampered by his preconceptions. William Morris associated the fire which both Dryden and Pope demanded from any translation of the Classical epics with antiquity of diction and the ring of the narrator's voice. In his version the "Aeneid", a poem designed for a highly cultivated audience and for the most formal recitation, becomes a tale of action such as might have been related around the fire in the depths of an Icelandic winter; and the Italian translations of D. G. Rossetti are similarly partial, since they select those features of the centuries before Raphael that agree best with the vague and languid pessimism of the pre-Raphaelite movement:

> Lo! I am she who makes the wheel to turn;
> Lo! I am she who gives and takes away;
> Blamed idly, day by day,
> In all my acts by you, ye humankind.

These lines, though allegedly based on a Canzone by Dante, in no way differ from the original poetry of Rossetti and his circle.

Robert Browning, on the other hand, in the foreword to his translation of the "Agamemnon" of Aeschylus, states that it is the translator's duty "to be literal at every cost save that of absolute violence to our language": a healthy prescription which he nullifies by granting himself in his next sentence "the use of certain allowable constructions which, happening to be out of daily favour, are all the more appropriate to archaic workmanship". Yet the rough-hewn English which he uses conforms to no language that ever has been in favour; it is a mock-Greek variant of Browning's own style which often, in its pursuit of literalness, does unpardonable violence to the English language, "Klutaimnestra's" speech to the "Choros", protesting against her exile, provides an example of this:

> Now, indeed, thou adjudgest exile to me,
> And citizen's hate, and to have popular curses:
> Nothing of this against the man here bringing,
> Who, no more awe-checked than as 'twere a beasts' fate,—
> With sheep abundant in the well-fleeced graze-flocks,—
> Sacrificed *his* child

Here the pedantic use of *popular* for *of the people*, and the curiously Germanic compound nouns and adjectives are more odd than archaic. Browning has invented his own Greek world and placed Aeschylus in it. Similarly, Gilbert Murray (1866–1959) a far more experienced scholar, in the early years of this century, found an equivalent for the Greek verse dialogue and chorus in the measures of Swinburne, and translated the same lines of Clytemnestra's speech into a clearer but none the less Victorian idiom:

> Aye, now, for me, thou hast thy words of fate;
> Exile from Argos and the people's hate
> For ever! Against him no word was cried,
> When, recking not, as 'twere a beast that died,
> With flocks abounding o'er his wide domain,
> He slew his child . . .

Murray finds it necessary to resort to a stock poetic idiom (*recking not, as 'twere*) in order to give the first of Greek dramatists majesty and temporal distance. A contemporary translator, Louis MacNeice (b.1907), by contrast, still pre-serves Aeschylus's hieratic dignity when translating the same lines into a timeless though hardly colloquial English:

> Now your verdict—in my case—is exile
> And to have the people's hatred, the public curses,
> Though then in no way you opposed this man
> Who carelessly, as it were a herd of sheep
> Out of the abundance of his fleecy flocks
> Sacrificed his own daughter . . .

MacNeice succeeds by allowing Aeschylus to speak for himself without "deviating into modern manners". A later generation may, however, accuse him of using the language of his own poetry and W. H. Auden's, in much the same way as Murray made use of Swinburne's, which he did to an even greater extent in translating Euripides than when confronted with the greater strictness of the "Agamemnon". The choruses of Murray's "Hippolytus" indeed, are in-distinguishable in manner from those of Swinburne's "Atalanta in Calydon":

> There riseth a rock-born river,
> Of Ocean's tribe, men say;
> The crags of it gleam and quiver,
> And pitchers dip in the spray:
> A woman was there with raiment white
> To bathe and spread in the warm sunlight,
> And she told a tale to me there by the river,
> The tale of the Queen and her evil day.

The most famous verse translation of the 19th century, Fitzgerald's "Rubaiyat of Omar Khayyam", has the advantage over these versions from the Greek, in that there was no original to which Fitzgerald (1809–1883) owed a debt of faithfulness. It is merely a Victorian poem in the oriental convention based on some quatrains by the Persian astronomer-poet, which in its use of personification, its

Dr. E. V. Rieu

C. K. Scott-Moncrieff (1889–1930)

From a portrait by Mercer in the Scottish National Portrait Gallery.

Arthur Waley

Constance Garnett (1862–1946)

over-capitalization, apostrophe and stock poeticism recalls all the worst features of minor Victorian poetry. Fitzgerald's Persia, despite his knowledge of the language, most forcibly recalls the divan-room in a 19th century furniture exhibition.

Morris, Rossetti, Browning, Murray and Fitzgerald adapted their authors' styles to their more or less erroneous pictures of the age in which these authors lived and worked. But a more general form of Victorian distortion was practised by lesser men, who were often good scholars, simply in order to underline the greatness of the work they were presenting. The more important the book in the cultural history of mankind, the more self-important the language in which it must be translated. Even "Don Quixote", which continually mocks at pomposities of verbiage and imagination, was subjected by its Victorian translators to a fatal process of verbal inflation. H. E. Watts, in his translation of 1888, shows himself a master of Cervantes' Spanish infinitely superior to Shelton and Motteux and their successor Smollett, who translated from the French. Yet in his awe before this mighty classic, he resorts to tortuous old-world language which turns Sancho from an earthy peasant into a pretentious clown. The squire is speaking the English of no known century when he protests to his master in these words against his rebuke for using too many proverbs:

> 'Fore God, Sir master of ours ... but your worship makes complaint of a mighty little thing. Why the devil should you fret yourself because I make use of my estate who have none other nor other stock in trade but proverbs, and more proverbs, and just now I have four that offer which come fit like pears in a pottle; but I will not say them for good silence is called Sancho.

Cervantes' colloquial tone has vanished, and Sancho's proverbs have become deliberately quaint. The Spanish is accurately followed, yet if the tale were told by a reincarnate author to a contemporary audience, the introductory apostrophe would certainly be shorter, and the number of dependent clauses fewer. My own solution in the Penguin "Don Quixote" is:

> "Goodness me, my dear master . . . you complain about very small matters. Why the devil do you fret yourself because I make use of my wealth? For I have no other. My only fortune is proverbs and still more proverbs. Why four of them occur to me now that come slick to the point, or like pears in a basket. But I won't say them for Sage Silence is Sancho's name." (II, 43)

Even this retains a slightly archaic tone, and the third and fourth sentences might read still more colloquially; "I've got nothing else. Proverbs and proverbs, that's my whole stock-in-trade."

This Victorian version of "Don Quixote" is on the whole less fusty than the equally scholarly "Arabian Nights" of Sir Richard Burton (1821–1890), which contains such pseudo-Arabic convolutions as the opening of the Second Kalendar's tale:

> Know, O my lady, that I was not born one-eyed and mine is a strange story; an it were graven with needle-graver on the eye-corners, it were a warner to whoso would be warned.

While at other moments the narrator observes with a pomposity equal to that of Watts' Sancho: "Then she stripped off her outer gear and Badr-al-Din arose and doffed his clothes."

The recent translations of a few of these tales by N. J. Dawood preserve the oriental flavour while avoiding the grotesque literalness of Burton. In the same way the excessive archaisms of the Victorian translators of Icelandic sagas, Sir George Dasent, William Morris and others, have been avoided in one or two recent renderings, such as Magnus Magnusson and Hermann Patsson's "Njal's Saga".[1]

[1] Penguin Books, 1960.

V

Victorian standards began to mend about the year 1871, which saw the publication of Benjamin Jowett's Plato. Though feeling compelled to convey the importance and the temporal distance of the philosopher by a somewhat ponderous vocabulary and sentence structure, Jowett (1817–1898) saw no need to archaize. Describing the captives in the cave at the opening of the myth in "The Republic", he wrote decently in the language of his century:

> And now, I said, let me shew in a figure how far our nature is enlightened or unenlightened:—Behold! human beings living in an underground den, which had a mouth open towards the light and reaching all along the den; here they have been from their childhood, and have their legs and necks chained so that they cannot move, and can only see before them, being prevented by their chains from turning round their heads. Above and behind them a fire is blazing at a distance, and between the fire and the prisoners there is a raised way; and you will see, if you look, a low wall built along the way, like the screen that marionette players have in front of them, over which they show their puppets.

Jowett renders the Greek accurately and with due Victorian dignity, yet fails to interpret for his reader those sentences which should reveal the exact topography of the cave. How, one asks, can a mouth "reach all along the den"? Is the wall, which is behind the prisoners, above or below the raised way? Such questions of interpretation no doubt seemed to Jowett to be beside the point. His duty as translator was to put the Greek into English, not to make good his author's oversights or explain his meaning to readers who could not grasp it, in whatever language they found him, as readily as those of his own day. To add this duty to that of plain translation has become the task of the 20th century craftsman. In rendering the same passage seventy years later (1941), F. M. Cornford not only put

Plato's Greek into more current English, but conveyed by his more exact choice of words, and with the aid of a couple of footnotes, the precise relation to one another of the fire, the captives, the wall and the raised way:

> Next, said I, here is a parable to illustrate the degrees in which our nature may be enlightened or unenlightened. Imagine the condition of men living in a sort of cavernous chamber underground, with an entrance open to the light and a long passage all down the cave.[1] Here they have been from childhood, chained by the leg, and also by the neck, so that they cannot move and can see only what is in front of them. At some distance higher up is the light of a fire burning behind them, and between the prisoners and the fire is a track[2] with a parapet built along it, like the screen at a puppet show, which hides the performers while they show their puppets over the top.

[1] The length of the "way in" (eisodos) to the chamber where the prisoners sit is an essential feature, explaining why no daylight reaches them.

[2] The track crosses the passage into the cave at right angles, and is *above* the parapet built along it.

Cornford has realised the scene and recreated it for his reader, who might not have known from the Jowett version that the captives faced the light, though at such a distance from it that none of it reached them, and that in front of them was a wall of the cave, for the track was a winding one.

Cornford's "Republic" is a typical of the work of our century, which did not seriously begin until after the first World War. The Edwardian era suffered from a Victorian hang-over. Even such accomplished work as Constance Garnett's in the field of Russian and William Archer's in his complete Ibsen (completed 1912) constantly reminds the reader or listener that the characters were speaking Russian or Norwegian, and that only thanks to the translator do we know what they said. Their coy pet names, absurd endearments and stiff sentiments underline their essential foreignness, which is rendered almost unnoticeable in more recent translations of the same novels and plays.

In contrast to the Victorians and Edwardians, whose antiquarian productions are, by a complete reversal of taste, now declared unreadable, craftsmen in the last twenty years have aimed principally at interpretation in current language, even at the risk of reducing individual authors' styles and national tricks of speech to a plain prose uniformity, a danger which they have just succeeded in avoiding in the best of their work. They have also, in common with most writers of their time, modelled their prose closely on common speech rhythms. Where Jowett wrote a convoluted style, rich in semi-colons and unrelated clauses but deficient in full-stops, Cornford reduced his sentences to a 20th century length, even at the cost of sometimes leaving the reader to decide, in default of a guiding conjunction, exactly what relation one sentence bears to another.

As scholarly as the Victorians, the moderns strive to satisfy the vastly increased public which has remained at school till the age of 18, or has taken university courses in non-linguistic subjects and cannot consequently be expected to be primarily concerned with literature. The new translator, therefore, aims to make everything plain, though without the use of footnotes since conditions of reading have radically changed and the young person of today is generally reading in far less comfortable surroundings than his father or grandfather. He has therefore to carry forward on an irresistible stream of narrative. Little can be demanded of him except his attention. Knowledge, standards of comparison, Classical background: all must be supplied by the translator in his choice of words or in the briefest of introductions.

The plain prose narrative has already been discussed in the case of "Beowulf". The first and pioneer exercise in this manner, however, was E. V. Rieu's "Odyssey" of 1946. True, the prose "Odyssey" of S. H. Butcher and Andrew Lang (1879) was among the most successful of Victorian translations. Their language however was ornate, literary, and sometimes as obscure as Browning's through clinging too closely to the phraseology and word-order of the Greek. W. H. Rouse's version is plainer, but lacks distinction and settled purpose. As a successful headmaster, Rouse appears to have addressed himself, perhaps involuntarily, to the young. Rieu, on the other hand, began with the intention of obeying what he himself calls "the principle of equivalent effect", that is to say to create in an adult audience the same impression as was made by the original on its contemporaries. For this reason, since tales today are no longer told in verse, he decided to translate Homer's narrative into contemporary prose. In fact his cadences, if not his choice of vocabulary, are poetic, and his rendering of the Homeric epithet, a stumbling-block to most translators, skilful and various. In his "Iliad", which followed his "Odyssey" four years later, he gave both pathos and eloquence to Priam's plea to Achilles, already quoted in Chapman's and Pope's versions:

> "Most worshipful Achilles", he said, "think of your own father, who is the same age as I, and so has nothing but miserable old age ahead of him. No doubt his neighbours are oppressing him and there is nobody to save him from their depredations. Yet he at least has one consolation. While he knows that you are still alive, he can look forward day by day to seeing his beloved son come back from Troy; whereas my fortunes are completely broken. I had the best sons in the whole of this broad realm, and now not one, not one, I say, is left. There were fifty when the Achaean expedition came. Nineteen of them were born of one mother . . ."

"The frame of mind in which we approach an author", wrote Matthew Arnold in his essay "On Translating Homer", "influences our correctness of appreciation of him; and Homer should be approached by a translator in the simplest frame of mind possible." Arnold further advises any would-be translator of Homer "not to trouble himself with constructing a special vocabulary . . . in obedience to any theory about the peculiar qualities of Homer's style".

Dismissing Chapman for his Elizabethan complexity and the "high intellectualisation" of Pope's version, also he leaves the field open for a future translator who "will have an eye for the real matter". Though Arnold postulated the English hexameter as the best medium and was unduly anxious that this ideal version should satisfy the scholars rather than the Greekless public, the "eye for the real matter" in preference to the manner was first shown by Rieu, who insisted that the "Odyssey", with its well-knit plot, its psychological interest, and its interplay of character, is the true ancestor of the long line of novels that have followed it.[1]

VI

Twentieth century translators, influenced by the spread of science-teaching and the growing importance attached to accuracy even to the exclusion of spirit have, I repeat, generally concentrated on prose-meaning and interpretation, and neglected the imitation of form and manner.

There is, however, a field in which the reverse is true. The translation of lyrical poetry, always the most exacting undertaking, has engaged a number of fine poets who have in the last years added considerable tracts to the territory familiar to the reader of English. Outstanding as pioneer is Arthur Waley (b.1889), whose *Chinese Poems* now represent for our time the poetry of a whole civilization which was scarcely known before, since the few conventionally translated lyrics that had appeared created very little impression. Faced with the alternative of imitating form or content, Waley unhesitatingly chose the latter. His English measure, a variety of stressed verse which owes something to the example of Gerard Manley Hopkins, was adopted as an equivalent and not as an approximate copy. "Each character in the Chinese", wrote Waley in a note to his *170 Chinese*

[1] Introduction to the "Odyssey", p. 10.

Poems of 1918, "is represented by a stress in the English; but between the stresses unstressed syllables are of course interposed." The translation is vouched for as literal, and where padding might have been necessary to fill out a line, Waley has preferred to vary his metre in order to avoid it. He omits rhyme, since it is impossible to produce the same rhyming effects as the Chinese. The prescription, as set out in this note on method, might seem unpromisingly dry. But, as Waley notes, "about two lines out of three have a very definite swing similar to that of the Chinese lines". The translator, in fact, being himself poet as well as scholar, has written poems which stand as such in their own right. The grandeur of language and the subtle changes in pace of 'The Bones of Chuang Tzu' by Chang Heng (A.D. 78–139) represents Waley at his highest level:

> I, Chang P'ing-Tzu, had traversed the Nine Wilds and seen
> their wonders,
> In the eight continents beheld the ways of Man,
> The Sun's procession, the orbit of the Stars,
> The surging of the dragon, the soaring of the phoenix in his
> flight.
>
> In the red desert to the south I sweltered,
> And northward waded through the wintry burghs of Yu.
> Through the Valley of Darkness to the west I wandered,
> And eastward travelled to the Sun's extreme abode
> The stooping Mulberry Tree.
>
> So the seasons sped; weak autumn languished,
> A small wind woke the cold.
>
> And now with rearing of rein-horse,
> Plunging of the tracer, round I fetched
> My high-roofed chariot to westward.
> Along the dykes we loitered, past many meadows,
> And far away among the dunes and hills.
> Suddenly I looked and by the roadside
> I saw a man's bones lying in the squelchy earth,
> Black rime-frost over him . . .

The whole poem is sustained on this level. Vast cosmo-logical prospects are narrowed to a single conversation with the dead man on the value of a recall to life, which he rejects. Many of the poems which Waley has chosen are shorter and more personal. Poets hitherto unknown in English, such as Po Chü-i and Li Po, are called back from their distant centuries to take modern form and yet preserve the individuality of their own lives and age.

Occasional successes in the same manner have been scored by Ezra Pound, in "The Seafarer" already mentioned, and by Robert Graves (b.1895) in his "Instructions to the Orphic Adept"—almost completely adapted from the Greek—and his versions of the Mexican poet, Juana de la Cruz. John Masefield, J. E. Flecker and Stephen Spender, among our poets in their own right, have produced a few translations of authentic merit. However, since Waley set the example, much more systematic work has been done by devoted verse-translators with a view to introducing known and unknown poets from abroad, if not in their entirety, at least in adequate selections. Here the late Norman Cameron's Villon, and J. B. Leishman's renderings of Rilke are out-standing. In undertaking to present a very large proportion of the Austrian poet's output, Leishman set himself a task in which he has perhaps achieved only an uneven success. Unlike Waley, he has not striven merely for an equivalent form. He has aimed at a complete imitation and, faced with Rilke's close-packed reasoning, has sometimes produced poems that fail to sing. Nevertheless, he has made it possible for a large public with no first-hand knowledge to catch something of Rilke's individuality. Certainly Rilke's con-siderable influence on English poetry of the last thirty years has largely been conveyed by way of the Leishman versions. Similarly, Hölderlin, a poet who presents almost equal problems of interpretation though rhythmically easier to transmute, has taken satisfactory English form in the versions of Michael Hamburger.

One poet who devoted much of his energy to translation

was Roy Campbell (1901–1957). Beginning with Baudelaire, who has so far defeated every Englishman who has
attempted him, Campbell went on to produce some uneven
and rather too colourful Lorca and a complete version of the
poems of St. John of the Cross, which cannot be bettered.
Campbell possessed a great lyrical strength and boldness,
and an almost Victorian power of writing not in single lines
but stanza by stanza. His opening of St. John's most famous
"En una noche oscura" has a remarkable authenticity, yet
carries over almost the full rhyme-scheme of the original:

> Upon a gloomy night,
> With all my cares to loving ardours flushed,
> (O venture of delight!)
> With nobody in sight
> I went abroad when all my house was hushed.
> In safety, in disguise,
> In darkness up the secret stair I crept,
> (O happy enterprise!)
> Concealed from other eyes
> When all my house at length in silence slept.

Campbell's mastery is complete both here and in many
single poems which he translated in the later years of his life
from the Spanish and the Portuguese. Campbell's taste was
individual; he enjoyed a rip-roaring poem even on a
spiritual theme, and avoided the subtleties of half thought
and shadowy emotion. Baudelaire's, in fact, was too subtle
and divided a mind for him, and Lorca's a little too sensitive.
So far English versions of Lorca have not been successful.
This was however true of St. John up to the moment when
Roy Campbell attempted him. The miracle of lyrical
translation takes place only when poet and translator are
almost evenly matched.

For this reason verse translations of Goethe, and particu-
larly of his *Faust*, have been until recently unsatisfactory.
However, in the last few years both Louis MacNeice and
Philip Wayne have produced readable and characteristically

racy versions of Goethe's poem. The defects of most Victorian translators of the play were that they endeavoured to bring over into English a high seriousness which was not present in the original. The best of them, such as that by the American Bayard Taylor, fail for that reason, and because of a quite un-Goethean obviousness in their rhymes. Mephistopheles, "prying around" in the Classical Walpurgis-night of Part II, reflects somewhat heavy-footedly in Taylor's version:

> And as among these fires I wander, aimless,
> I find myself so strange, so disconcerted:
> Quite naked most, a few are only shirted;
> The Griffins insolent, the Sphinxes shameless,
> And what not all, with pinions and with tresses,
> Before, behind, upon one's eyesight presses!—
> Indecency, 'tis true, is our ideal,
> But the Antique is too alive and real . . .

Compared with this version, Wayne's leaps briskly into life, with no *poetic* verbiage or syntactical awkwardness:

> Now, as I wandered through the fields of flame,
> I'd much to vex me, much to disconcert:
> Naked the lot, just here and there a shirt,
> The sphinxes brazen, griffins without shame;
> The crowd of creatures, winged and tressed, displays
> No end of back and front views to the gaze . . .
> We, lewd at heart, can relish the salacious,
> But this antique's too lifelike and vivacious.

Wayne on the whole keeps it up, as indeed does MacNeice also, from whom it would be easy to quote equal felicities.

Of similar accomplishment to Wayne's Goethe is a work not strictly in the field of translation, the modernised *Canterbury Tales* of Nevill Coghill, which have restored the speed and immediacy of the original, now lost owing to the ordinary reader's need to look up or remember the meaning for Chaucer's time of phrases that have either lapsed from the language or acquired different significance. Less well-known than Coghill's Chaucer is a similar and somewhat earlier modernization of Langland's *Vision of Piers Plowman* by Henry W. Wells (1938). Wells, a skilful modernizer, does not strain away the flavour of the ancient language though he effectively removes the linguistic difficulty of reading 14th century dialect. Another alliterative poem of the same epoch which presents difficulties to the modern reader, *Sir Gawain and the Green Knight*, has also been rendered into more contemporary English by Brian Stone. It is indeed now possible to read most of the masterpieces of the 14th century without undue puzzlement as to meanings.

Other attempts to naturalize into English tracts of poetry hitherto unknown to those without linguistic accomplishment, include collections of Russian poems made by Professor Maurice Bowra, who has himself contributed a number of splendid translations in full rhyme and exact metre of poems by writers of the revolutionary epoch, in particular of "The Twelve" by Alexander Blok, and of "I believe sang the guns and the squares" of Viktor Khlebnikov. Among the most interesting adaptations from the Russian, however, have been versions of the 19th century poet Fyodor Tyutchev, made by one of our most accomplished younger poets, Charles Tomlinson in collaboration with the Russian and English scholar Henry Gifford. The method of this small collection intrinsically differs from those of previous lyrical translators. The intention is to re-write the essentials of the poem in English, transferring it from its own century into our own, and choosing metres and rhyme-schemes suitable to the new poem but in no way matching the old. The endeavour would seem over-bold. Yet on comparing Tomlinson's versions with the Russian one discovers that new poems have been created and nothing of the originals has been sacrificed except so much as would have made them seem trite derivatives from the German romantics if brought across in the conventional way.

> I knew her erst in days afar
> That full of fairy fancies are . . .

are the opening lines of a Tyutchev lyric rendered by Sir Cecil Kisch. This translation catches all the qualities in the Russian poet which bind him to his century. Tomlinson, on the other hand, lifts him into ours:

> Neither thought not threat
> But a limp and sullen sleep
> This night-sky gloom
> Clouded from every quarter.
> Only the intermittent flare as
> Lightnings, deaf-mute demons
> Converse with one another.

This opening of a short lyric conveys the essence of Tyutchev, the sense of living nature and its menaced beauty that gave him so strong an influence over Boris Pasternak. Several attempts have been made to present selections from this great poet of modern times, but so far without outstanding success. Herbert Marshall's versions of his contemporary, Vladimir Mayakovsky, on the other hand, catch the pulsing speed and vigour of a man whose personal violence made him for a short time the laureate of the Revolution. Marshall's version of his poem on the suicide of Yessenin has all the colloquial ease of Philip Wayne's Goethe in a higher concentration:

> You have passed,
>   as they say,
>   into worlds elsewhere.
> Emptiness . . .
>   Fly
>   cutting your way into starry
>   dubiety,
> No advances,
>   no pubs for you there.
> Sobriety.

No, Yessenin,
                this
                        is not deridingly,—
in my throat
            not laughter
                        but sorrow racks
I see—
        your cut-open hand
                        lingeringly
swings
        your very own bones
                        like a sack.

Marshall catches to perfection the mixture of curtness, defiance, poeticism and mock-poeticism that went to the making of this remarkable poet.

A final mention must be made of the American poet W. S. Merwin, a recent resident in this country, whose versions of a selection of the traditional Spanish *romances* has for the first time conveyed their individual quality into English. Previous translators since the 18th century had rendered them in English ballad metres, with plangent rhymes to correspond with the alliterative half-rhymes of the Spanish. Merwin, on the other hand, catches the colloquial convention and the unobvious singing quality of the *romance*, as in that most beautiful fragment, "The Prisoner":

It was May, the month of May,
When warm days are with us,
When the grain gets its growth
And the fields are in flower,
When the skylark sings
And the nightingale gives answer,
When those who are in love
Go in love's service,
Except for me, wretch living
In sorrow in this prison,
Not knowing when it is day

Nor when night has come
Except for a little bird
Which sang to me at dawn;
A man killed it with a crossbow,
God give him an ill reward!

It was almost certainly the example of Arthur Waley that prompted this group of poets to make more or less free versions of foreign writers to whom they felt specially attuned. In this way we have acquired a number of extensions to our own rich store of poetry, which have in varying degrees impressed and influenced the poets who are writing today.

VII

It was Rieu's example, however, and not Waley's that set a number of distinguished writers, of talents equal to those of the Elizabethan translators, to the work of retranslating the great works of the past for a 20th century audience. Robert Graves, Rex Warner, Philip Vellacott, Michael Grant, Aubrey de Sélincourt and W. F. Jackson Knight are among the outstanding practitioners of the new "plain prose" method which, upon examination, however, proves to be not a single method, like that of the Elizabethans, but to vary from the direct telling of a somewhat mannered story in Graves's version of Apuleius's "Golden Ass" to a radical expansion which brings out all the telescoped meanings and sub-meanings of the Latin in the case of Jackson Knight's "Aeneid". Verse is rendered in free verse forms by Vellacott and in prose by Jackson Knight. A strict following of Rieu's example is attempted by none.

The contrast between the Elizabethan and the 20th century method is most marked in the case of "The Golden Ass". William Adlington in his translation of 1566, intro-

duced the witch Meroë, the cause of all the hero's mis-
fortunes, with a conversational and slightly Euphuistic
prolixity suitable for leisurely reading aloud:

> And so I fortuned to come to the house of an old woman that sold
> wine, called Meroë, who had her tongue sufficiently instructed to
> flattery: unto whom I opened the causes of my long peregrination
> and carefull travell, and of myne unlucky adventure; and after I
> had declared unto her such things as then presently came to my
> remembrance, shee gently entertained mee and made mee good
> cheere; and by and by beeing pricked by carnall desire, she brought
> mee to her own bed chamber.

Robert Graves writes for a reader in the train or on a
holiday beach. Reducing the whole matter to its bare
narrative bones, he says rather more—he is using a different
text—in a quarter less words:

> I went to an inn run by a woman named Meroë. She was no longer
> young but extraordinarily attractive, and when I told her my sad
> story and explained how anxious I was to return home after my
> long absence, she pretended to be deeply sympathetic, cooked me
> a grand supper for which she charged me nothing, and afterwards
> pressed me to sleep with her.

Graves claims the licence to "alter the order not only of
phrases but of sentences, where English prose logic differs
from Latin",[1] and to avoid the use of footnotes brings their
substance into the story itself whenever it reads obscurely.
He remains true, however, to the tone if not to the complex
language of his original, as he does also in his version of
Suetonius's "Twelve Caesars". When he grows impatient
with his author, on the other hand, he sharply alters the tone
and drops into irony at his expense. When Graves comes to
Lucan's evocation of the witch Erichto in the sixth book of
the "Pharsalia", he parodies rather than elucidates Lucan's
baroque talent:

[1] *The Golden Ass*, Introduction, p. 11.

> Witches have introduced the art of dragging the stars from the sky; and know how to turn the moon dim and muddy-coloured, as though she were being eclipsed by the Earth's shadow—after which they pull her close to them and torture her until she secretes poisonous foam on the plants growing underneath.

This reads like a translation of one of the odder anecdotes from Pliny. It not only reduces exalted poetry to humble prose, but obliterates all the poetic content of the original. "Secretes" not only fails to correspond to the Latin, but suggests a modern scientific primer, while "to catch and bottle whatever lightning happened to fall", a few lines further on, makes the whole idea of witchcraft, in which Lucan believed, appear ridiculous.

At the opposite end of the scale Jackson Knight gives a more formal and detailed account of Aeneas's vision of the dead Hector than Dryden's version already quoted:

> It was the hour when divinely-given rest first comes to poor human creatures, and creeps over them deliciously. In my sleep I dreamed that Hector stood there before my eyes. He looked most sorrowful, and was weeping plenteous tears. He was filthy with dust and blood, as he had been that day when he was dragged behind the chariot, and his feet were swollen where they had been pierced by the thongs. And, oh, how harrowing was the sight of him; how changed he was from the old Hector, back from battle wearing the spoils of Achilles, or that time when he had just flung Trojan firebrands onto the Greek ships! Now his beard was ragged and his hair clotted with blood, and all those wounds which he had sustained fighting to defend the walls of his homeland could still be seen.

Using more words even than Dryden—and twice as many as Virgil—Jackson Knight gives an exact rendering of his original, in plain and pleasing prose though with considerably less grace than Rieu in his Homer, or Graves in "The Golden Ass".

More strictly comparable to Dryden's is the verse "Aeneid" of C. Day Lewis (b.1904) which although as uneven in its language as Graves's Lucan conveys some of the sweep though not all the majesty of Virgil's poem. But Day Lewis is happier in his version of the "Georgics", which are more capable of translation in the homespun style of the contemporary poet who no longer aims at the epic grandeur postulated by Arnold.

Two recent verse translations of Dante's "Commedia", one by Laurence Binyon (1869–1942) and the other by Dorothy Sayers—the latter left incomplete at her death—fail for another reason to be completely satisfactory. The effort to sustain Dante's *terza rima* is in both cases heroic. Binyon, allowing himself more metrical freedom, comes closer to poetry, and at times writes fine passages. But the slightly pre-Raphaelite prose version of Thomas Okey better represents the essential simplicity of Dante's style and the complexity of his thought.

Standards of modern translation are extremely high, and the competence with which plays and novels with extremely up-to-date dialogue are rendered in unaffected English is quite remarkable. "Translaterese", the legacy of the Victorian amateur, has almost entirely disappeared. Here Scott Moncrieff's Proust set the example, which has been followed by Gerard Hopkins in his versions of Mauriac and other French novelists, by Edwin and Willa Muir in their magnificent versions of Kafka, by Eithne Wilkins and Ernst Kaiser in Robert Musil's novels, by Henry Reed and Archibald Colquhoun in various plays and novels from the Italian, and by David Magarshack and Rosemary Edmonds in their retranslations of familiar novels from the Russian.

In addition, much has been done in the last twenty years in the field of more specialized translations, such as those of the complete works of Freud and Jung, to provide what must be, in effect, official versions which will represent these most important thinkers in the wide regions where English is read in preference to German has necessitated the recruiting of translators not only skilled in their craft but well acquainted with the subject-matter of their originals. Theology too has attracted translators with more than literary talents capable of rendering the abstruse thought of such men as Kierkegaard, Heidegger and Karl Barth. The English translator has, in fact, in these fields the double responsibility of writing well and of representing his author's meaning so accurately that there shall be no appreciable difference between the English and the original. In this most exacting task a very high level of success has been achieved.

Much work of the past also has been presented afresh to the English-reading public in a form suitable to the straight-forward requirements of this century. The next may, as E. V. Rieu expects, demand that the whole task be done over again to meet its different conventions. For the life of a translation rarely exceeds a hundred years, and those few which achieve greater longevity owe the continued favour of their readers to their intrinsic merits rather than to their faithfulness. We do not now turn to Dryden's "Aeneid" or Pope's "Iliad" in order to make acquaintance with Virgil and Homer, but value them as the greatest long poems of their own age. Future generations may read Rieu's "Odyssey" and Graves's "Golden Ass" as examples of first-rate 20th century writing, even when fashions of translation have radically altered once more. The translators of this mid-century may then be generally compared, as they have been in this essay, to the masters of the first Elizabethan age.

Ashton-under-Lyne
Public Libraries

ENGLISH TRANSLATORS AND TRANSLATIONS

A READING LIST

I

General Works:

PREFACE TO OVID'S EPISTLES, by John Dryden (1680)
—included, with other material concerning translation, in W. P. Ker's 2 volume edition of Dryden's Essays, Oxford, 1926.

AN ESSAY ON TRANSLATED VERSE, by the Earl of Roscommon (1684; enlarged 1685).

ESSAY ON THE PRINCIPLES OF TRANSLATION, by A. F. Tytler (Lord Woodhouselee) (1791)
—included in Everyman's Library, 1907.

ON TRANSLATING HOMER, by Matthew Arnold (1861).

MODERN TRANSLATION, by E. S. Bates. Oxford (1936).

INTERTRAFFIC: STUDIES IN TRANSLATION, by E. S. Bates (1943).

ASPECTS OF TRANSLATION (1958)
—No. 2 in 'Studies in Communication' published by the Communication Research Centre, University College, London.

THE READER'S GUIDE, edited by W. Emrys Williams (1960)
—includes 'Classics in Translation' by E. V. Rieu, with special references to Penguin translations.

BOOKMAN'S MANUAL: A GUIDE TO LITERATURE, by B. Graham (9th ed. revised by H. Hoffman, New York, 1960)
—a standard handbook which includes numbers of translations by British and American translators.

THE ENGLISH BIBLE, A HISTORY OF TRANSLATIONS, by F. S. Bruce (1961)

II

¶ *A select alphabetical list of authors and translations, including the principal versions referred to in the text of the essay:*

AESCHYLUS
Works Translated by L. Campbell, 1890
    "   Gilbert Murray, 1920-39
    "   Philip Vellacott, 1956 and 1961

Agamemnon	,,	Robert Browning, 1877
		(Included in John Murray editions of Poetical Works, 1896 and 1919)
	,,	Louis MacNeice, 1936
Prometheus Bound	,,	Rex Warner, 1947

APULEIUS
Metamorphoses   Translated as "The Golden Asse" by William Adlington, 1566

Reprinted, revised by S. Gaselee, 1915

Translated as "The Golden Ass" by Robert Graves, 1950

THE ARABIAN NIGHTS   Translated by John Payne, 1882–89

,,   Richard Burton, 1885–6

,,   N. J. Dawood, 1954 and 1957 (a small selection in two volumes, entitled "The Thousand and One Nights" and "Aladdin").

ARIOSTO
Orlando Furioso   Translated by Sir John Harington, 1591

BALZAC
Cousin Bette   Translated by Kathleen Raine, 1948
Cousin Pons   ,,   ,, Norman Cameron, 1950
Domestic Peace and Other Stories   Translated by M. A. Crawford, 1958
Lost Illusions   ,,   ,, Kathleen Raine, 1951
Old Goriot   ,,   ,, M. A. Crawford, 1951

BEOWULF   Translated by William Morris and A. J. Wyatt, 1895

,,   C. K. Scott Moncrieff, 1921

,,   G. D. Bone, 1946

(Prose versions) J. R. Clark Hall, Revised C. L. Wrenn, 1950

David Wright, 1957

THE BIBLE
The Wyclifite Bible   Translated by John Wyclif and his followers from the Latin Vulgate, 1384, and improved and revised, 1396.

The New Testament	Reprinted, 1848, by Charles Whittingham from the 14th century translation manuscript. *From the original texts:*
The New Testament (1525) revised (1534) and *The Pentateuch* (1530)	Translated by William Tyndale. The Pentateuch and the New, Testament reprinted from the edition of 1534, in the 'Matthew Bible', 1537 and the 'Great Bible', 1539.

Miles Coverdale's translation of the whole Bible, 1535

The Authorized Version, which was the work of 47 Scholars, 1611

The Revised Version (New Testament, 1881 and Old Testament, 1885)

The New Testament	Translated into modern English by James Moffat, 1913
The Old Testament	Translated into modern English by James Moffat, 1924
The Gospels	Translated by E. V. Rieu, 1952
Acts of the Apostles	Translated by C. H. Rieu, 1957
	„ „ J. B. Phillips, 1955 as 'The Young Church in Action'

The New English Bible, the New Testament only in modern English, Oxford and Cambridge, 1961

BOETHIUS

De Consolatione Philosophiae	Translated by Geoffrey Chaucer, and included in standard editions of his Works.
	Translated by 'I.T.', revised by H. F. Stewart, Loeb Library, 1918.

LUIS DE CAMOES

The Lusiads	Translated by R. Fanshawe, 1655
	„ „ Leonard Bacon, New York, 1950
	„ „ W. C. Atkinson (prose version) 1952

CERVANTES

Don Quixote	Translated by T. Shelton, 1612-20. Reprint edited by J. Fitzmaurice Kelly, 1896
	Translated by Peter Motteux, 1700-12. Reprinted in Everyman's Library, 1933
	Translated by C. Jarvis, 1742, and frequently reprinted
	„ „ T. Smollett, 1755
	„ „ J. Ormsby, 1885

Translated by H. E. Watts, 1888 and 1895
,,   ,, J. M. Cohen, 1950

CHEHOV
Works   Translated by Constance Garnett, 1916-1922
The Cherry Orchard,   ,,   ,, Elisaveta Fen, 1951, 1954
Three Sisters, Ivanov,   reprinted in one volume 1959
The Seagull, Uncle
Vania, The Bear, The
Proposal, A Jubilee

CHINESE POETRY
Chinese Poems   Translated by Arthur Waley, 1946. The collection includes the greater part of "*170 Chinese Poems*", 1918, "*More Translations from the Chinese*", 1919, and "*The Temple*", 1923. Paper-back edition 1961.

DANTE
The Divine Comedy   Translated by H. F. Cary, 1805-1814. Reprinted in Everyman's Library, 1955
Prose Translation facing original:
Inferno by J. A. Carlyle, 1900
Purgatorio by Thomas Okey, 1900
Paradiso by P. H. Wicksteed, 1899
Translated by Laurence Binyon, 1933-43
,,   ,, Dorothy Sayers, *Hell*, 1949
,,   ,, Dorothy Sayers, *Purgatory*, 1955
,,   ,, Dorothy Sayers and Barbara Reynolds, *Paradise*, 1962

DOSTOYEVSKY
Crime and Punishment,   Translated by David Magarshack, 1952-58
The Devils, The Idiot,
The Brothers Karamazov

EURIPIDES
Works   Translated by A. S. Way, Loeb Library, 1912, translation facing text
Alcestis, Bacchae,   Translated by Gilbert Murray, 1902-15
Electra, Hippolytus,
Iphigenia in Tauris,
Medea, Trojan Women
and Rhesus

Alcestis, Iphigenia in Tauris and Hippolytus   Translated by Philip Vellacott, 1953

Ion, Women of Troy, Helen, The Bacchae   Translated by Philip Vellacott, 1954

FROISSART

Chronicles   Translated by Lord Berners, 1901–3. (Edited W. P. Ker, The Tudor Translations)

GOETHE

Faust: Parts I and II   Translated by Sir Theodore Martin, 1865–87. Reprinted in Everyman's Library, 1954
Translated by Philip Wayne, 1949-59
Abridged and translated by Louis MacNeice, 1951

Scenes from the Faust of Goethe   Translated by P. B. Shelley, included in Poetical Works, 1905

GOGOL

Dead Souls   Translated by George Reavey, 1949
     ,,   ,, David Magarshack, 1961

HOMER

The Works   Translated by George Chapman, 1611-16, edited Allardyce Nicol, 1957

The Iliad and *The Odyssey*   Translated by Alexander Pope, 1715-25, (*The Iliad*, reprinted in World's Classics, 1902-3 and frequently reprinted)
Translated by William Cowper, 1791
Prose translation by W. H. Rouse, 1937-8 (as 'The Story of Achilles' and 'The Story of Odysseus')
Prose translation by E. V. Rieu, 1945 and 1950

The Iliad   Prose translations by A. Lang, W. Leaf and E. Myers, 1883; by Samuel Butler, 1898

The Odyssey   Prose translations by S. H. Butcher and A. Lang, 1879; by Samuel Butler, 1900; by T. E. Shaw (T. E. Lawrence), 1935

IBSEN

The Pillars of the Community, The Wild Duck, Hedda Gabler   Translated by Una Ellis-Fermor, 1950

Rosmersholm, The Master Builder, John Gabriel Borkman	Translated by Una Ellis-Fermor, 1958
Enemy of the People The Wild Duck Rosmersholm	Translated by I. W. MacFarlane, 1960

KAFKA

The Castle	Translated by Willa and Edwin Muir, 1930
The Great Wall of China	,, ,, ,, ,, ,, ,, 1933
The Trial	,, ,, ,, ,, ,, ,, 1937
In the Penal Settlement	,, ,, ,, ,, ,, ,, 1949

LUCAN

Pharsalia	Translated by Nicholas Rowe, 1718
	Prose translation by Robert Graves, 1956

MOLIÈRE

The Misanthrope, The Sicilian, Tartuffe, A Doctor in Spite of Himself, The Imaginary Invalid	Translated by John Wood, 1959

MONTAIGNE

The Essays	Translated by John Florio, 1603
	Reprinted in Everyman's Library, 1910
	Translated by Charles Cotton, 1685
	,, ,, E. J. Trechmann, 1927
A Selection	Translated by J. M. Cohen, 1958

OMAR KHAYYAM

The Rubaiyat	Translated by Edward Fitzgerald, 1859
	4th edition, revised, 1879

PLATO

The Works	Translated by Benjamin Jowett, 1871
The Republic	Translated by F. M. Cornford, 1941
The Republic	Translated by H. D. P. Lee, 1955
Gorgias	Translated by W. Hamilton, 1960
The Last Days of Socrates	Translated by Hugh Tredennick, 1954
The Symposium	Translated by W. Hamilton, 1951

PLINY THE ELDER
The Natural History Translated by Philemon Holland, 1601 as "The Historie of the World"
A Selection Edited by Paul Turner, 1962

PLUTARCH
Lives Translated by Sir Thomas North, 1579, from the French of Jacques Amyot
 Collective translation edited by John Dryden, 1683-6
 Edition revised by A. H. Clough, 1864
 Reprinted in Everyman's Library, 1910
Six Roman Lives Translated as "Fall of the Roman Republic" by Rex Warner, 1958
Nine Greek Lives Translated as "The Rise and Fall of Athens" by Ian Scott-Kilvert, 1960

PROUST
Remembrance of Things Past Translated by C. K. Scott Moncrieff, 1922-30
 Completed by Stephen Hudson, 1931

QUEVEDO
The Visions Translated by Sir Roger L'Estrange, 1667

RABELAIS
Gargantua and Pantagruel Translated by Sir T. Urquhart (Bks. 1-3) and Peter Motteux (Bks. 3-5), 1653-94
 Reprinted in Everyman's Library, 1929
 Translated by J. M. Cohen, 1955

SCHILLER
Wallenstein Translated by S. T. Coleridge, 1800
 Included in the Poetical Works, 1828 and later editions.

SOPHOCLES
Works Translated by L. Campbell, 1883
Oedipus King of Thebes, Antigone, Wife of Heracles, Oedipus at Colonus Translated by Gilbert Murray, 1911-48
Theban Plays Translated by E. F. Watling, 1947
Electra, The Women of Trachis, Philoctetes, Ajax Translated by E. F. Watling, 1953

STENDHAL

The Charterhouse of Parma	Translated by C. K. Scott Moncrieff, 1926
	,, ,, M. R. B. Shaw, 1958
Scarlet and Black	Translated by C. K. Scott Moncrieff, 1927
	,, ,, M. R. B. Shaw, 1953

TASSO

Gerusalemme Liberata	Translated as "Godfrey of Bulloigne or The Recovery of Jerusalem" by Edward Fairfax, 1600
	Reprinted H. Morley, 1890

TOLSTOY

Works	Translated by Louise and Aylmer Maude in World's Classics, 1906–47
Anna Karenin	Translated by Constance Garnett, 1901
	,, ,, Rosemary Edmonds, 1954
The Death of	Translated by Constance Garnett, 1902
Ivan Ilyich	Translated by Rosemary Edmonds, 1960
War and Peace	Translated by Constance Garnett, 1904
	,, ,, Rosemary Edmonds, 1957
The Cossacks, Happy Ever After	Translated by Rosemary Edmonds, 1960

TURGENEV

Works	Translated by Constance Garnett, 1894–99
First Love	Translated by Isaiah Berlin, 1950

VIRGIL

Works	Translated by John Dryden, 1697
The Aeneid	Translated by William Morris, 1875
	Translated by C. Day Lewis, 1952
	Prose translation by W. F. Jackson-Knight, 1956
The Georgics	Translated by C. Day Lewis, 1940
The Pastoral Poems	Translated by E. V. Rieu, 1949

820.9